GENGHIS KHAN

AND THE BUILDING OF THE MONGOL EMPIRE

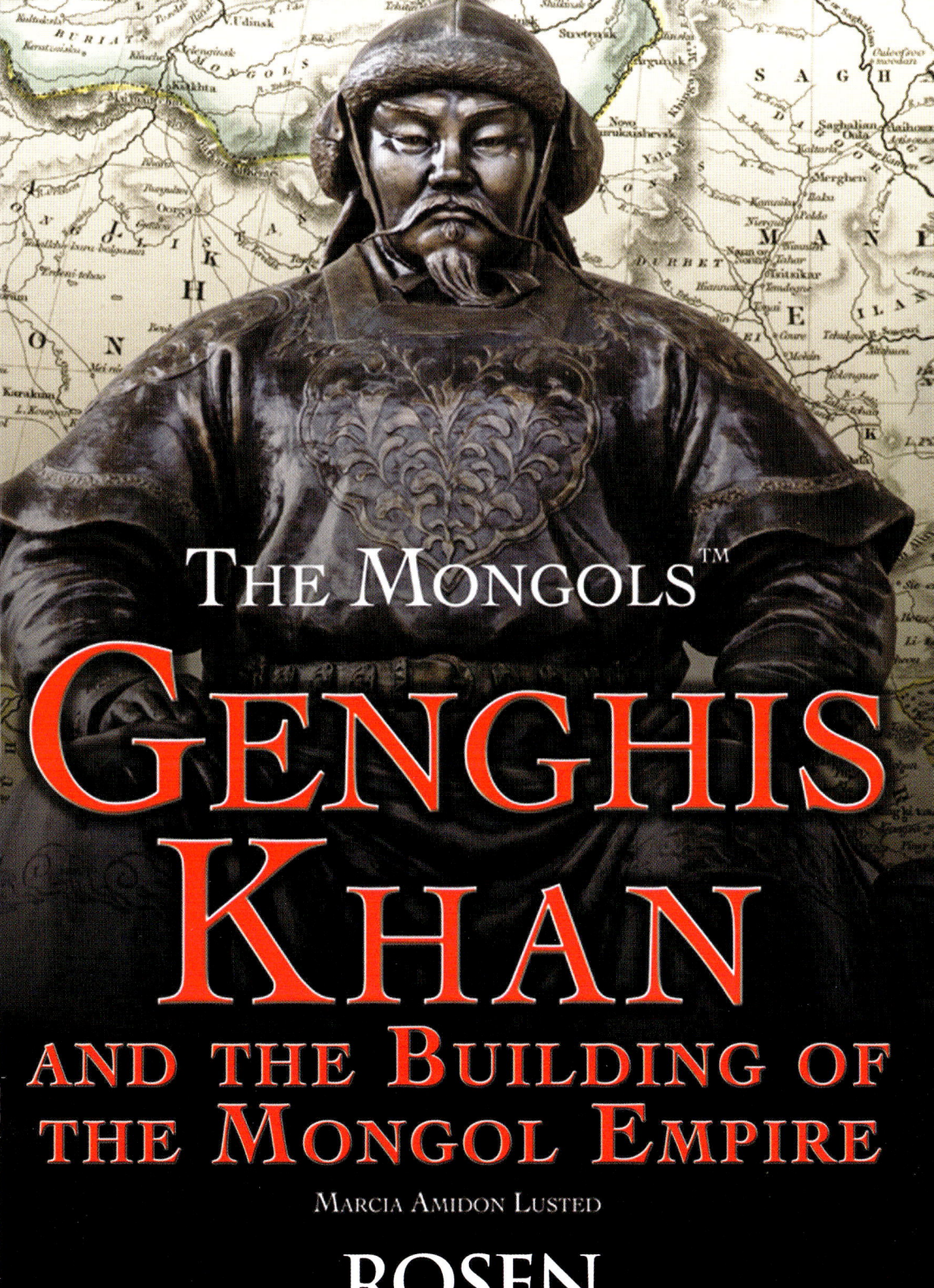

THE MONGOLS™

GENGHIS KHAN
AND THE BUILDING OF THE MONGOL EMPIRE

MARCIA AMIDON LUSTED

ROSEN PUBLISHING
New York

Published in 2017 by The Rosen Publishing Group, Inc.
29 East 21st Street, New York, NY 10010

Copyright © 2017 by The Rosen Publishing Group, Inc.

First Edition

All rights reserved. No part of this book may be reproduced in any form without permission in writing from the publisher, except by a reviewer.

Library of Congress Cataloging-in-Publication Data

Names: Lusted, Marcia Amidon, author.
Title: Genghis Khan and the building of the Mongol Empire / Marcia Amidon Lusted.
Description: New York : Rosen Publishing, [2017] | Series: The Mongols | Includes bibliographical references and index.
Identifiers: LCCN 2015047668| ISBN 9781499463521 (library bound) | ISBN 9781499463507 (pbk.) | ISBN 9781499463514 (6-pack)
Subjects: LCSH: Genghis Khan, 1162–1227. | Mongols—Kings and rulers—Biography. | Mongols—History.
Classification: LCC DS22 .L87 2016 | DDC 950/.21092—dc23
LC record available at http://lccn.loc.gov/2015047668

Manufactured in China

Contents

Introduction..6

Chapter 1
A Boy Named Temujin....................................10

Chapter 2
Rising to Power..20

Chapter 3
The Rule of Genghis Khan..............................28

Chapter 4
Creating an Empire.......................................37

Chapter 5
The Mongol Empire.......................................46

Glossary..55

For More Information...................................57

For Further Reading......................................59

Bibliography..60

Index...62

Introduction

It is the largest plain in the world, stretching 5,000 miles (8,047 kilometers) from Hungary in the west to Manchuria in the east. This plain, known as the steppes, has always been a place where many different nomadic groups of people traveled and interacted. The grassy plains were easy to travel across on horseback. The few mountain ranges were not impossible to cross. Routes developed across the steppes to carry trade goods from the East to Europe. Ideas, languages, styles, and cultures also mixed and spread across these plains.

The climate of the steppes could be very harsh, especially in the north. This part of the steppes bordered Siberia in the north and the Gobi Desert in the south. Winters could last nine months, with extreme cold. The -40 degree Fahrenheit (-40 degree Celsius) temperatures were in contrast to summer temperatures that could reach more than 100 degrees Fahrenheit (38 degrees Celsius). It was also very dry, making it almost impossible to farm. This forced the tribes to wander. At first they hunted. Then they herded animals like horses, goats, cattle, camels, and sheep as a way to keep themselves fed. They could also trade their animals for other goods that they needed such as grain, metal, pottery, and cloth.

Many different tribes inhabited the steppes. Many were herding tribes, who lived on the open grasslands and herded animals from place to place. Some tribes lived in more wooded

A horse grazes on a grassy plain of the Mongolian steppes.

areas farther north and hunted for their survival. The Mongols called their area Sibr, the source of the name "Siberia." They lived in hunting camps, wore animal fur, and used sleds pulled by dogs or reindeer for transportation because horses could not survive so far north. Their lifestyles were very different from those of the plains tribes.

The steppes in the twelfth century, when the boy who would one day become Genghis Khan was born, were not an easy place to live. A shaman named Teb Tengri later reminded

Genghis Khan's sons of what life was like before he came to power, saying:

> *Everyone was feuding. Rather than sleep they robbed each other of their possessions. Rather than rest they fought each other. In such a world one did not live as one wished, but rather in constant conflict. There was no respite, only battle. There was no affection, only mutual slaughter.*

The many tribes that wandered the steppes were often at war, causing constant violence and chaos. Since they were skilled at warfare, they often raided settled towns or other tribes to take the things that they needed. Since they didn't stay in one location, their alliances were not based on living in one place. They frequently fought with each other. Even the tribes themselves, such as the Mongols and the Tatars, often fought with their own members. Tribes dissolved and reformed. Kidnappings and murders were common as leaders struggled for control of their tribes.

Everyday life could also be very hard. There was extreme poverty, especially in places where food did not grow well. Some people were forced to eat roots and mice to stay alive. Travelers to Mongolia wrote that the people there would eat anything they could, including wolves, foxes, dogs, and even lice. Those tribes that herded animals used them for food, either as meat or for their milk. Sheep also provided wool for clothing and for their homes. These homes were movable structures called yurts or gers. They were six-sided tents supported by a wooden frame. The tentlike part of the yurts was made of felt. The entire structure could be collapsed and folded up for travel. This was very important in a culture where tribes routinely moved from one place to another according to the seasons or for better hunting.

It was into this difficult and complicated way of life that Temujin, who would later be known as Genghis Khan, was born. He would one day be one of the most powerful leaders the world has ever known, but first his life on the steppes would shape who he was and how he behaved. Life was hard, but the people who lived in those conditions became stronger because of it.

Chapter 1
A Boy Named Temujin

No one is exactly sure when Temujin was born, since the Mongols at that time had no written language and so did not keep any written records. Temujin is believed to have been born around the year 1162. His mother, Hoelun, had been kidnapped by his father, Yesugei, during a hunting trip. This was a common practice among the steppe tribes. According to *The Secret History of the Mongols*, a history of the Mongol people that one of Genghis Khan's sons had commissioned many years later to keep his father's memory alive, Yesugei was entranced by Hoelun's beauty. However, it was more likely that he simply needed a wife. By Mongol custom, she had to be obedient to him. Yesugei and Hoelun formed a family clan that was part of a larger group of clans that lived together. Yesugei became the leader of these allied clans.

A Boy Is Born

Hoelun's first child, Temujin, was born on a hillside near the Onon river. Supposedly he was born clutching a large blood clot the size of a knucklebone in the fingers of his right hand. This was a sign, or prophecy, that he would be a great leader, although it did not say if he would be good or evil. He was

A BOY NAMED TEMUJIN

This familiar portrait of Genghis Khan was painted on silk using ink and watercolors.

named after a great warrior who had been killed in battle by Yesugei just before the boy's birth. Yesugei already had two sons by a previous wife. Hoelun had four more children after Temujin.

Growing Up as a Mongol

Along with his many siblings and his half-brothers, Temujin learned to ride horses. Most Mongol children could ride without help by the time they were four, since horses were so important to the Mongol way of life. He also learned to hunt and fish. His best friend was named Jamukha. He played with Temujin and his brothers. Jamukha and Temujin eventually became *andas*, or blood brothers. They exchanged gifts, with

White Bone and Black Bone

In Temujin's time, Mongolian society was arranged according to a strict system of kinship. Each lineage, which was the family line of people descended from a common ancestor, was called a bone. White bone lineages were lineages where people were related closely to each other, so they were not allowed to intermarry. Lineages that included more distant relatives, with whom intermarriage was allowed, were called black bone lineages. White bone lineages could also claim to be descended from Mongol princes. They were of a higher social level than black bone lineages.

Jamukha giving Temujin a whistling arrow (with an arrowhead carved so that it whistled when launched) and Temujin giving Jamukha an arrow carved from juniper wood. They swore an oath of loyalty to each other and drank from a cup where a few drops of each one's blood had been mixed. This bond was even stronger to Mongols than that of real brothers.

Mongol boys were married at the age of nine. However, until they were older, their marriage was more like an extended engagement. Marriages were a common way to create

Temujin, like all Mongol children, learned to ride at a very early age.

alliances between clans and families. They could also improve the reputation of a family. The accepted practice among Mongol tribes was for the betrothed boy to move into the camp of his future bride's family. He would work as a laborer or apprentice until he was old enough to support a family on his own. Then he and his new wife would return to his family's camp.

A Twist of Fate

Temujin was betrothed to the daughter of a man named Dei the Wise. He told Yesugei that he had a dream about Temujin and that he would one day be a great leader. He was eager to have his daughter Borte married to Temujin. Yesugei traveled with Temujin to Dei's camp and left him there to remain with Borte's family. Then Yesugei headed home to his own camp.

If Yesugei had made it home safely, Temujin might have spent his life as a traditional Mongol nomad with a family, the same as any other young man of his time. But on his way home, Yesugei met a group of men from a Tatar tribe. This was another of the nomadic tribes that wandered the steppes. According to steppe custom, strangers were always offered hospitality, so Yesugei was welcomed to join them for a meal. Unfortunately, they had recognized him as someone who had robbed them in the past. Tatars and Mongols were also sworn enemies. They poisoned Yesugei's food, and when he finally reached his home camp, he was close to death.

After Yesugei died, Temujin was called back home from Borte's family camp, with the idea that he would lead the group of clans in his father's place. But the other clan leaders did not want to be led by such a young boy. It was customary for the brothers of a dead man to take his wife. But Hoelun already had too many children, and Yesugei's brothers did not want the responsibility for such a large family. The tribe abandoned Temujin's clan, taking their valuable animals and leaving Temujin alone with just his mother, his four siblings, his two half-brothers, and a family servant. With winter approaching and no source of food, it was a death sentence.

OUTCASTS

Life became very hard for Temujin's small family clan. Without animals like horses or sheep for food, they were forced to live off the land, eating plants and scavenging for roots and berries just to stay alive. Needles were bent into fishing hooks, and the younger children used wooden arrows tipped with sharpened bones to hunt for small animals.

One day Temujin and his brother Kasar went fishing. They managed to catch a fish, but their two half-brothers snatched it away and ate it themselves. Because the family was living in such desperate conditions, even the loss of a fish might mean a smaller chance of survival. Temujin took his bow and arrow and shot one of his half-brothers to death. He pardoned his other half-brother, and they eventually became close friends.

MAKING DECISIONS, MONGOL STYLE

When a Mongol clan or tribe needed to make important political or military decisions, the members gathered in a tribal council known as a *kurultai*. The word "kurultai" comes from the Mongolian root *khur*, meaning "to gather," and *ild*, meaning "together." They were often held for the election of a new khan or a big decision such as going to war. Families, clans, and individuals voted simply by showing up: if they agreed with a decision, they came, and if they disagreed, they stayed away. Since most of the people of the steppes lived in widely scattered groups, it was an important occasion when a khan,

Even today, people in central Asia sometimes make important decisions by meeting in a kurultai, or tribal council. At this kurultai in Kyrgyzstan, people called for the resignation of the Kyrgyz president.

or chief, called for a kurultai. It was at one of these gatherings that Temujin was elected Genghis Khan, or Grand Khan, of the Mongols. Kurultai are still held today in some central Asian countries.

Temujin was already demonstrating the personality traits that would enable him to rule as Genghis Khan. He was ruthless to his enemies but kind and generous to those who were loyal to him.

A Captive at Camp

Over the next few years, Temujin's family managed to survive. He himself had many things happen to him, such as being kidnapped by the Taichiud clan. Because Temujin's killing of his half-brother took place on their land, the Taichiud felt it was their responsibility to punish him for it. They also did not want Temujin starting any fights with neighboring tribes that were under Taichiud control. After a party of warriors entered Temujin's camp to take him, he fled to the mountains but was eventually captured.

He spent several weeks in captivity at a Taichiud camp. He was forced to wear a device called a cangue, which looked like a yoke for oxen. It allowed him to walk but didn't allow him to feed himself or drink water. The Taichiud families had to take care of his basic needs. The members of the Taichiud

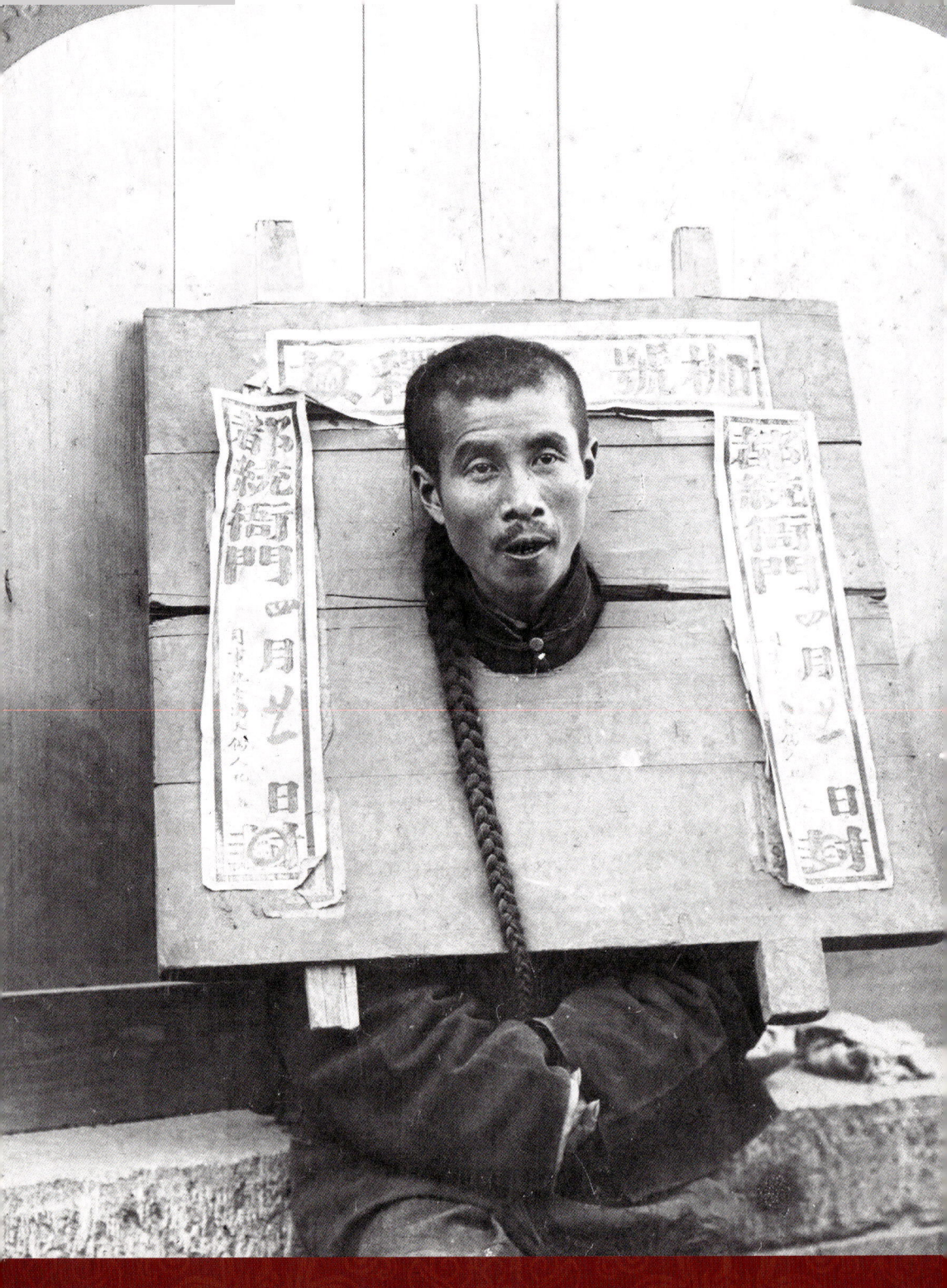
A Chinese prisoner wears a cangue, similar to the one worn by Temujin when he was captured by the Taichiud.

camp were from different backgrounds and of different social standings. Some had also come to the camp as prisoners of war, now forced to be servants. One of these servant families came to Temujin's aid, removing the cangue at night so that he could sleep. Eventually they helped him escape by giving him a horse and food. Again Temujin learned about rewarding loyalty and judging people by their actions toward him, instead of how they were related to him or how high their social standing was. This was a very different idea from traditional Mongol society and one that would shape Temujin as a leader.

Becoming an Adult

Temujin arrived back home. At sixteen, he was a man, and he was also ready to lead his family clan. He had not seen Borte, his fiancée, in seven years, and it was time for them to marry. Temujin went in search of her family's camp and found that she was still waiting for him, even though at seventeen she was past the usual age when she should have gotten married. He brought his new wife back to his family camp, ready to start his own family and strengthen his clan.

Chapter 2
Rising to Power

Temujin and his family had survived being outcast by their clan alliance. Now Temujin was a grown man with a wife. He was ready to take on the full responsibility of ruling his own small clan. The group had already grown with the addition of two young men, Bo'orchu and Jelme. Bo'orchu had befriended Temujin when Temujin went to reclaim several horses that had been stolen from his family and the two became companions. Jelme had been given by his father to Temujin as a foster son and servant. The number of people over whom Temujin ruled in his small group was already growing.

More Strife

Unfortunately, the group was not destined to have a peaceful life. In the world of the steppes, there was constant strife. People had long memories for wrongs that had been inflicted on them and their clans. Raids and attacks—intended to gain political power, to acquire goods, or for revenge—were frequent. Soon, Temujin's small group was attacked by the Merkit tribe, which overran their camp. Temujin's clan did not have enough members to successfully resist the Merkits, so they fled the camp and hid in the forest. However, Temujin's wife, Borte, was not so lucky, and she was captured by the Merkits and taken to their camp, where she became the wife of the Merkit leader.

This fifteenth-century Persian illustration shows Genghis Khan seated on a throne, with his wife, Borte, by his side.

Temujin was determined to recover Borte. With the help of Toghril, who was a sworn blood brother of Temujin's father, and also with help from his own blood brother, Jamukha, they raised an army strong enough to attack the Merkit camp. It was the first time that Temujin commanded an army. Though he had fewer warriors than the Merkit forces, he was victorious. Borte returned to the camp and to her role as Temujin's wife. Borte later gave birth to Temujin's first child, a son named Jochi.

Alliances and Arguments

Temujin and Jamukha renewed their childhood friendship. Temujin was able to make alliances with other clans, along with Jamukha and Toghril, and the three of them ruled over an increasingly large number of Mongol clans. This partnership between Temujin and Jamukha lasted for almost two years, until an incident that split them apart. It started out as a simple disagreement as to where was the best place to camp: near the mountains, which was better for the horses, or next to a mountain stream, which was better for the shepherds and their livestock. This small disagreement ultimately led to splitting the group into two parts, one commanded by Temujin and the other by Jamukha. The clan members were forced to choose which leader they would follow. Temujin promised the Mongols who followed him that if they swore loyalty to him, he would lead them to glory. The number of men who were now loyal to Temujin grew every year. Temujin's men included those who were descendants of the first khans, the title given to hereditary rulers and chiefs of Mongol tribes.

At the age of twenty-seven, Temujin decided to seek the title of khan and hopefully unite the many different Mongol clans into one tribe with one leader, something that had not been possible for many years. He called a kurultai of his followers and was elected as the new khan. Temujin, now the khan of his tribe, also hoped that his new title would attract some of Jamukha's followers and perhaps also force

ONG KHAN

Toghril, who was also known as Ong Khan, was one of Temujin's greatest protectors, but later he became Temujin's rival for power. Toghril had been a blood brother to Temujin's father, Yesugei. As a young man, Temujin strengthened his relationship with Toghril by giving him a valuable gift, a sable fur coat that was Borte's dowry. Toghril accepted the gift and treated Temujin as a son. Temujin accepted Toghril as his adopted father. As a result of the gift, Toghril not only gave Temujin and his clan protection but also a leadership role over other young warriors. It also elevated his standing among the other people of the steppes. When Temujin's wife Borte was kidnapped by the Merkits, Toghril told him, "In gratitude for the sable cloak, I will find your Borte for you, even if I have to destroy all of the Merkits."

Jamukha into a final contest for leadership of the Mongol people. Of course, both Temujin Khan and Jamukha (who had declared himself to be the *gurkhan*, chief of all chiefs) were still ruled by Toghril (also known by his title of Ong Khan), leader of the Khereid tribe. Ong Khan allowed the two younger men to rule over their separate groups because their conflicts with each other and the divisions they caused made it easier for Ong Khan to keep controlling all the Mongols.

Learning to Be Khan

As khan, Temujin was beginning to establish how he would rule his people, and some of his methods would be very different from what the Mongol people and the Mongol enemies were used to. He created a structure of power within his tribe that relied on the skill and loyalty of his men rather than simply family ties. The khan traditionally lived in a complex of yurts called the *ordu*. There, his family members made up a type of aristocracy over the rest of the tribe.

But Temujin Khan decided to structure his ordu by assigning important responsibilities to those who were loyal to him

Traditional yurts made from animal hides are still used in Mongolia today.

and had specific skills. The highest positions, as personal assistants to him, he assigned to Bo'orchu and Jelme, who had been loyal to him for more than ten years. He also established a system of guards, who were expert swordsmen and archers, to protect the herds of animals, the camp, and the khan himself. He also considered the men who butchered meat for meals to be an important defense, since Temujin Khan remembered how his own father had been poisoned and feared that the same thing would happen to him. This system of guards and protections would be used no matter where the ordu was located, allowing Temujin Khan to maintain his power at all times.

A New Order

Temujin was skilled in three things: he was a good military general, he knew his men well, and he was a great organizer. He gave his followers tasks based on what they did well, rather than the old system of assigning roles according to someone's social standing. He also knew that the most important responsibility for a group of nomads living on the steppes was to guarantee that their sources of food, their equipment, and their horses were always protected. He also required strict obedience to his commands, no matter what.

Ruling on the Move

In modern armies, the idea of a mobile command headquarters is common. During war or other military expeditions, a command center is quickly set up according to an established process. However, at the time of Temujin Khan, this was a new idea. Before him, the khan's command center, or ordu, was simply a loose collection of yurts and a hierarchy of people based only on their family relationships and social standing. Temujin Khan realized that he could not be an effective leader unless he had a system for setting up an ordu quickly and according to a specific structure. In a culture that spent most of its time on the move, without established cities or palaces, this was vital to both protecting the leader and making it possible to plan and launch attacks no matter where the army traveled. This, along with the organization of the army itself, was part of what made Temujin Khan such an effective leader.

Temujin Khan commanded his army from his royal tent, part of an ordu.

Successes and Failures

Over the next ten years, historians believe that Temujin did not have a smooth reign. Horses were stolen. Fighting broke out between Temujin and Jamukha. Temujin even may have been defeated and possibly exiled to China. Because there were no written records at the time, and *The Secret History of the Mongols* tells only the stories of Genghis Khan's successes and skips over this period of time, it is not certain what occurred.

However, by the year 1198, Temujin Khan had been restored to power, he and Toghril had successfully defeated the Tatar tribe, and Temujin's tribe itself had defeated the Taichiud clan. He was on his way to defeating his old enemies and gaining even greater power, but first he would have to defeat his oldest and strongest allies and rivals: Jamukha and Toghril.

Chapter 3
The Rule of Genghis Khan

By 1198, Temujin was once again growing more powerful. But he still faced two rivals in power: his blood brother, Jamukha, and his adopted father, Toghril. Tensions had risen between Temujin and Jamukha until Jamukha finally gathered an army to march against Temujin. On the steppes, no alliance was stable, and Temujin also persuaded Toghril to join forces with him against Jamukha. Even though Jamukha and Toghril had been allies, Toghril agreed to join Temujin and they planned a battle to take place at Koyiten. However, a severe snowstorm struck and both armies were unable to move because of the snow, so the battle was called off. This turned out to be an advantage for Temujin's army because as they withdrew from Koyiten, they were able to attack the Taichiud clan, who were loyal to Jamukha. Temujin defeated them in a fierce battle.

Defeating the Tatars

Temujin then went on to attack the Tatar clan, and in 1202, he successfully defeated them. They had been responsible for the death of his father, as well as the destruction of the old kingdom of the Mongols. Their defeat was a great accomplishment for Temujin. But at the same time, Toghril,

This illustration from a fourteenth-century Persian book shows Temujin Khan fighting the Tatars.

who was growing old and tired, was convinced by his son that it was better not to be an ally of Temujin's. Toghril decided to launch a plot to assassinate Temujin, but his plans were overheard and reported to Temujin, who then moved his army to a safer location. As he rode east, suddenly an army appeared in front of him, with Toghril and Jamukha leading it. Once again, alliances shifted, and Temujin was forced to flee with his army since they were so outnumbered. But as he fled, he encountered many other friendly tribes who decided to join him, rebuilding his army.

Later, Temujin and his men surrounded Toghril's camp at night and defeated them with a surprise attack. After a three-day battle, Toghril was defeated. Most of his tribesmen were slaughtered or joined Temujin's tribe. Toghril himself escaped but was later killed by a patrolling tribesman. Temujin then dealt with Jamukha, defeating him and his allied clans of Mongols and the Naiman tribe. Jamukha survived, but he would never be powerful again. After surviving for a while as a bandit, Jamukha turned himself in to Temujin. Because they had been blood brothers, Temujin was willing to pardon Jamukha, but Jamukha knew there was no place for him in Temujin's service. He asked to be executed, and Temujin granted his request, then buried his bones with honor.

THE NEW GREAT KHAN

The battle for control between Temujin, Jamukha, and Toghril was now over, and Temujin was the leader. In 1206, a great kurultai was held, and many of the people of the steppes attended. There, Temujin became Genghis Khan, "Universal Ruler," the emperor of "all who lived in felt tents," the people of the steppes.

Now that Genghis Khan had defeated his enemies, he focused on building stability for his empire and his people. He wanted his empire to last, since the steppes had previously been a place of chaos and constant warfare. Genghis Khan's method for creating stability and longevity was to put into place a new system. It would unite the empire and prevent small tribal leaders from fighting each other and weakening the empire overall. He divided his empire

Temujin is elected as the Great Khan, with his sons Ogedei and Jochi by his side.

into ninety-five military units, and each unit was responsible for maintaining one thousand warriors. The commanders of the military units were loyal men personally chosen by Genghis Khan. During times of war or conflict, each commander was expected to immediately assemble his one thousand men, and every man over the age of fifteen was required to serve military duty.

A New Code of Laws

Genghis Khan had other means of ensuring that his kingdom stayed united under his rule. He created more powerful offices within his organization, including administrators and chief justices. He abolished hereditary titles, meaning that sons no longer inherited leadership from their fathers. This would also help to stop small tribes and clans from fighting each other.

Organizing an Army

The organization of Genghis Khan's army was not his alone. It was based on an ancient method of organization used by the nomads of central Asia, and it was organized according to the decimal system, in units of ten. The largest group was the *tumen*, a unit of ten thousand men. This was divided into ten *mingghan* with one thousand men each. Each mingghan contained ten *jaghun* with one hundred men each, and the jaghun was divided into ten *arban*. The unit commanders were men who had proven their loyalty to Genghis Khan and so were considered to be the highest level of society.

Genghis Khan orders the punishment of a prisoner by whipping, as set out in his code of laws.

Genghis Khan also established a new code of laws, called the Yassa. The Yassa did not come from some existing code of laws or from a spiritual authority. Genghis Khan had his adviser Tata-tonga create the code, since he himself was illiterate, and allowed it to be written down because it was necessary to send it to all of his kingdom.

Some of the laws included in the Yassa were:

- Women could not be kidnapped or sold into marriage.
- Stealing animals was punishable by death.
- Hunting was forbidden from March to October so that wild animals could breed.
- Slavery of other Mongols was forbidden.
- All religions were to be treated with respect.
- Those people who provided essential services, such as doctors, lawyers, and teachers, did not have to pay taxes.
- The property of someone who died without heirs did not revert to the khan. Instead, it went to the person who had looked after the deceased.

Many of these laws are now basic tenets of law in countries around the world, but in Genghis Khan's time, they were new ideas. The Yassa worked to eliminate petty wars

The Written Word

Before Genghis Khan, there were no written records of Mongol history. Genghis Khan himself was illiterate, but he understood that it was important to establish a system of writing to make sure that his laws and wishes would be preserved exactly as he made them and would not be changed in the future. It was also important for keeping the administrative records of his kingdom. His adviser Tata-tonga also convinced him that official documents should be marked with an official seal to show that they were legal documents ordered by Genghis Khan. Tata-tonga became the official Keeper of the Great Seal to mark documents. Mongolian records were written in Uyghur script, a kind of writing that came from the Aramaic language. It was written from top to bottom and in columns going from left to right.

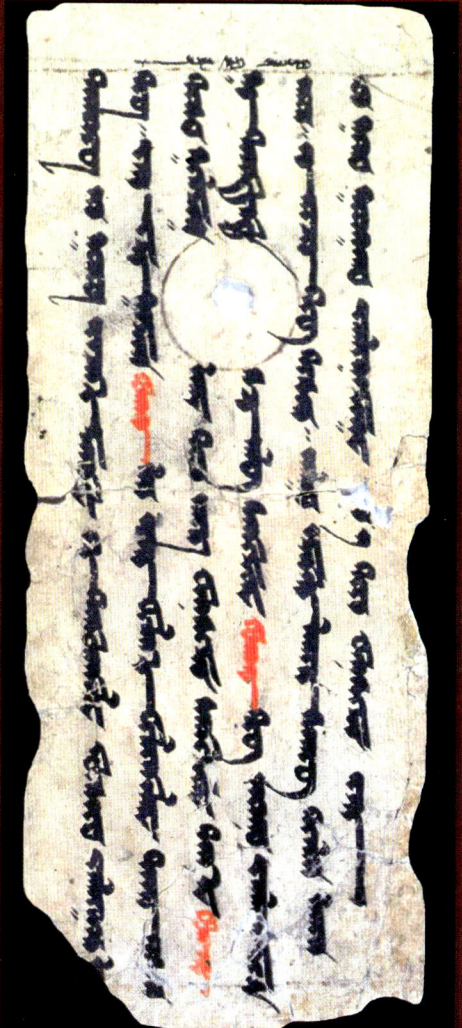

This manuscript is written in Uyghur script.

and sudden raids, to prevent most theft, and to allow the common Mongol tribesmen and their families to live in peace. Genghis Khan also established a census, allowed for the development of a system of written records, and gave foreign diplomats immunity.

    Genghis Khan had established himself as a supreme ruler. He had created a new structure and new laws for his kingdom. Now he would turn his attention toward the borders of his Mongol kingdom and aim to expand his control.

Chapter 4
Creating an Empire

As emperor of Mongolia, Genghis Khan now ruled over almost a million people. He had established new laws and a new government structure. The most powerful Mongol shaman (a holy man) had declared that Genghis Khan was the representative of Mongke Koko Tengri ("Eternal Blue Sky"), the Mongols' supreme god and that it was his destiny to rule the world. Genghis Khan himself supposedly said to one of his enemies, "I am the flail of God. If you had not committed great sins, God would not have sent a punishment like me upon you."

Genghis Khan, Conqueror

With his own kingdom firmly established, Genghis Khan began looking toward the countries that shared his borders. Historians have various theories on why he thirsted to conquer other lands. Perhaps all the wars in Mongolia had reduced the supply of animals and he needed to raid other countries to keep his people from starving. The increasing population would have made this necessary. It could be that weather conditions—perhaps a drought or very wet weather—forced him to look for new lands for the Mongol people. Or perhaps he felt that he had a divine right to conquer the world and rule over it.

Rain: A Secret Weapon

New evidence uncovered by scientists suggests that the Mongol army's success may have been aided by an unusual period of warm weather and plenty of rain. Scientists sampled tree rings in Siberia and were able to use them to create an accurate chronology of climate conditions between 1211 and 1225. Trees grow more under good weather conditions, creating wider rings. In drought conditions, rings are narrower. Previously, historians thought that Genghis Khan and his army were suffering harsh conditions in Mongolia and thus looking for food elsewhere. But if they were actually experiencing unusually warm and wet weather, then there would be plenty of grass for livestock and their warhorses. With plenty of horses for their conquests and food to fuel the army, the climate provided an ideal setting for Genghis Khan to build his empire beyond his homeland.

Tree rings can show changes in climate that took place over many years.

Commanding an Army

Genghis Khan had also created an army that was trained and ready for invasion. He used an extensive network of spies. He sent them out months before an attack to check defenses and map roads and escape routes. They would also determine where the enemy received its supplies. All of this could be valuable information to use against an enemy when attacking them.

Mongols were expert riders who fought on horseback using bows and arrows.

Genghis Khan was also quick to adopt any new technologies that he saw his enemies using. His own army of eight thousand warriors was controlled by a signal system of smoke and burning torches. Drums and flag signals were also used to relay commands. A group of swift riders and an established network of relay stations helped make sure that different parts of the army could communicate quickly over longer distances.

The soldiers themselves were well equipped with bows, arrows, shields, daggers, and lassos. They also carried food, spare clothing, and tools in their saddlebags, which could also be inflated and used as life preservers when they needed to cross deep rivers. And because Mongol warriors were expert horsemen who could control their horses using only their legs, their hands were free to shoot their bows and arrows. The army also had its support system. Oxcarts carried food, military equipment, people skilled in medicine, shamans, and government officials to record any captured valuables.

BATTLES IN CHINA

Genghis Khan's first campaign beyond his borders was against Xi Xia, the capital of the Tangut kingdom in northwestern China. He wanted to invade the empire of Jin, but he needed to conquer the Tangut capital to keep that army from attacking the flank (rear) of his army as they traveled to Jin. To reach Xi Xia, the Mongol army had to cross 200 miles (322 km) of the Gobi Desert and then march another 400 miles (644 km). The major battle took place in a mountain pass, where the Mongols pretended to retreat until the Tangut army left its fortified camp. Then the Mongol army turned back and conquered the enemy. This victory gave Genghis Khan control of the Silk Road oasis that was located there, as well as many tax revenues. He also brought thousands of Xi Xia craftsmen and artists back to Mongolia to help build his capital city of Karakorum.

After successfully capturing Xi Xia, Genghis Khan invaded the empire of Jin in northern China. Jin, with its twenty million people, was already involved in a war with the Chinese. Its huge army was trapped at the southern border, fighting the Chinese army, leaving the rest of the country vulnerable to attack. In 1211, Genghis Khan left for Jin with seventy thousand men. He supposedly said to his people, "Heaven has promised me victory."

The Mongol army made it through the Great Wall of China and conquered the capital city of Zhongdu (near the modern city of Beijing). This campaign gave Genghis Khan's men valuable experience in attacking a city that was completely protected by walls 40 feet (12 m) high. The Mongols developed new tactics for situations like these. They used catapults to fling diseased animal carcasses, large stones, and even flaming balls of naphtha (a flammable sticky pitch made from distilling cola tar and peat) over the walls. They would isolate the city and cut off supplies so that the inhabitants slowly

MACHINA VERSILIS

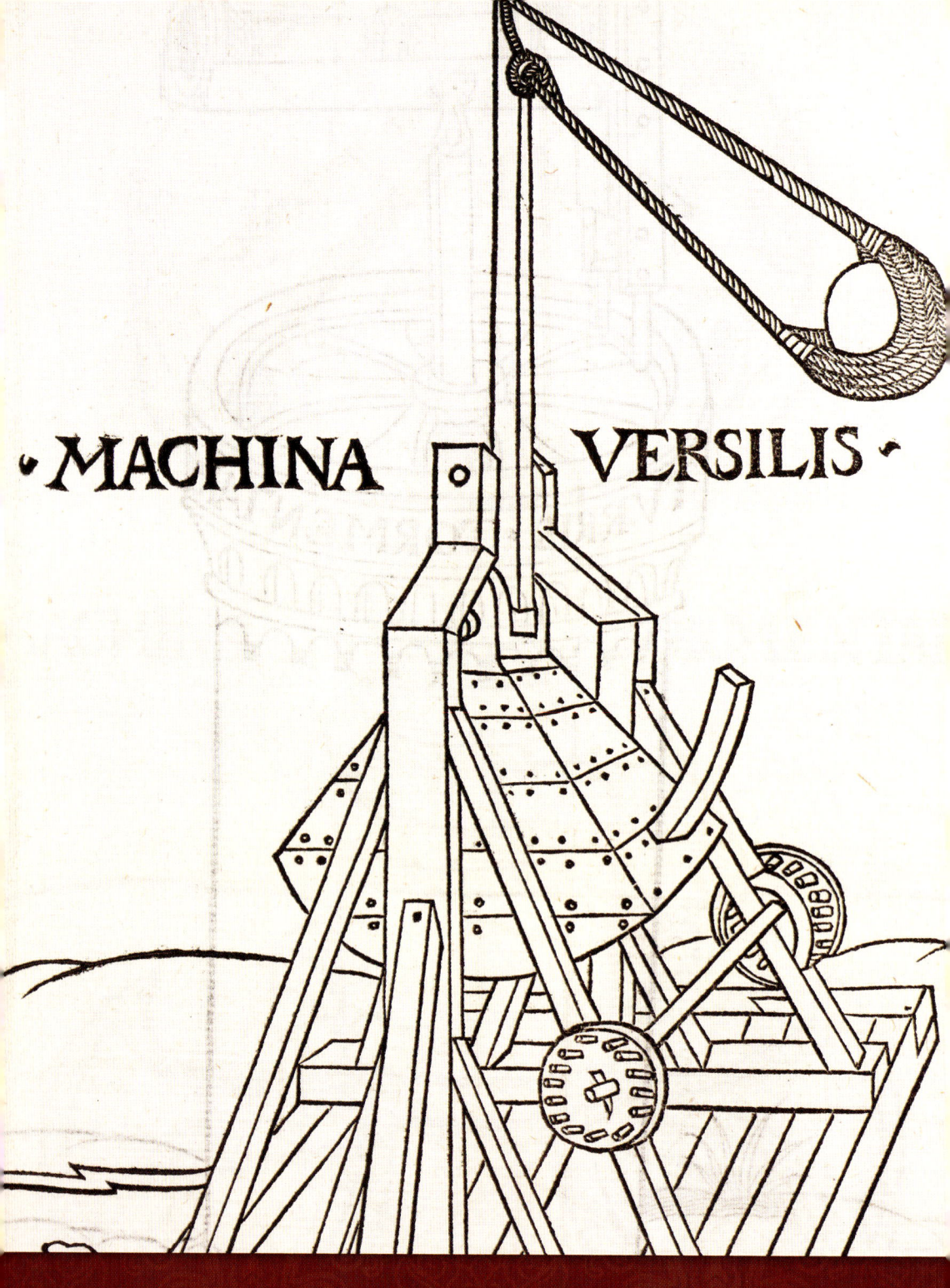

The Mongols used trebuchets like this one to fling large stones and other damaging objects at their enemies.

starved. They might dam or reroute a stream so that it flooded the town. They even made mannequins out of straw that resembled Mongol soldiers and placed them on horseback to make their army appear larger than it really was. Extra campfires also gave the impression that there were more soldiers camped outside the city than there actually were. The Mongols then used catapults and trebuchets to break down the city walls.

The Jin emperor finally offered Genghis Khan gold, silver, and one of his princesses if he would call off the attack. However, when the emperor moved his capital south to Kaifeng in 1214, Genghis Khan suspected that he might be reorganizing for an attack. He attacked Zhongdu again, stole the imperial treasure, and completely destroyed the city. Many years later, a traveler to Zhongdu was told that a white hill near the city was made from the bones of those killed in the Mongol attack.

Diplomacy and Death

Genghis Khan was also turning his attention toward his western borders and the Muslim countries beyond them. At first, he established trade with the Khwarizm dynasty, which included Turkestan, Persia, and Afghanistan. But this relationship crumbled when a Mongol official, on a diplomatic mission, was attacked because he was suspected of being a spy. When Genghis Khan demanded that the official responsible be sent

Siege Weapons

One of the strengths of Genghis Khan's leadership was his ability to see what worked well for enemy forces in warfare and adapt it for his army's use. The trebuchet, which is a type of catapult, was a technology adapted from the Chinese. A projectile, such as a rock, was placed in the weapon's arm, and then warriors would use a rope to pull the arm backward and put tension on it. When released, the projectile would fly through the air. It was especially effective for launching stones at city walls to break them down.

The Mongols also adapted the Chinese siege crossbow. It could shoot large arrows, including those with tips that were lit on fire, across long distances. It had three bows that were cranked back by a winch, giving the arrows more power than arrows launched by human archers.

Siege crossbows could shoot large arrows over very long distances.

to him for punishment, the Khwarizm leader refused and also sent back the head of the Mongol official.

Genghis Khan was so angered by this that he unleashed a three-part attack against the Khwarizm dynasty in 1219. These attacks were ferocious. Two hundred thousand Mongol warriors swept through cities, killing the people there. Those who were not killed in the initial attacks were forced to march ahead of the Mongol army as human shields for the next attack. Even small animals and other livestock were killed. It is said that the skulls of men, women, and children were piled in huge pyramids in the captured cities. Eventually, the shah of Khwarizm and his son were both captured and killed, ending the dynasty.

The attacks on Khwarizm helped to create Genghis Khan's reputation as a fierce, cruel, bloodthirsty warrior and leader. And his conquests continued as the Mongol Empire grew.

Chapter 5
The Mongol Empire

Genghis Khan had created an empire and an army that were powerful and far-reaching. He had conquered the Xi Xia kingdom and the Jin kingdom. He had pushed into the territory of the Khwarizm dynasty and conquered that as well, while increasing his reputation as a cruel and ruthless military leader.

He had also created a new system for governing his people and controlling his huge army. By creating laws that set out a rule for every situation and circumstance, and firm penalties for every crime, he was able to control his warriors and the millions of people he ruled over.

A Thirst for More

However, Genghis Khan was not satisfied with the territories he had already conquered. He continued to move into other countries. In 1218, he directed one of his generals to lead an attack against the Mongol state of Kara-Khitai, whose leader was a prince from the Naiman tribe. Genghis Khan had once defeated this tribe, and he felt that the new state was his rival. His general took twenty thousand horsemen to Kara-Khitai, captured and beheaded its prince, and added one more kingdom to Genghis Khan's empire.

This fourteenth-century Persian illustration shows Genghis Khan and his army in a battle against the Chinese in a mountain pass.

The Mongol army went on to destroy some of the great trading centers of the Silk Road, in today's Afghanistan and Iran. While the tales recorded of these conquests are probably exaggerated, cities that refused to surrender to Genghis Khan were shown no mercy. Genghis Khan supposedly told one of his generals, when told of a revolt by the inhabitants of the city of Herat in Afghanistan, "Since the dead have come to life, I command you to strike their heads from their body." Legend says that only forty of the city's inhabitants survived.

Reaching Toward Europe

At the same time, more of Genghis Khan's generals were defeating armies in Russia and Europe. More stories were told of the Mongol brutality, including one about two Mongol generals having dinner on top of a box, inside of which three captured Russian princes suffocated to death. Genghis Khan himself had been in India, considering a conquest of all of northern India. However, the hot, humid climate was not a good environment for Mongols, who were more accustomed to fighting in cooler, drier climates. Their horses also got sick, and their bows did not seem to work as well in the new climate. Genghis Khan decided to take his army back to Afghanistan, a more comfortable climate.

Genghis Khan was approaching sixty, an age that many Mongols of his time never reached. He became more and more concerned about how long he would live and who would take over for him when he was gone. He heard of a renowned Chinese monk, Ch'ang-ch'un, who practiced the Taoist religion. His name meant "eternal spring," and he was rumored to be three hundred years old. This monk supposedly knew the secret to immortality, which came from the famous "philosopher's stone." Genghis Khan sent for the monk, who would travel with one of the Mongol advisers. The monk met with Genghis Khan in 1222, after a very long journey, but when he was asked if he knew the secret to living forever, he told Genghis Khan that there was no such medicine to make men immortal. The monk stayed with the Mongol leader and later taught him about the Taoist religion. In 1223, the khan fell from his horse during a hunt and was nearly killed by a wild boar, and Ch'ang-ch'un urged him to take better care of himself. Still, Genghis Khan would not give up his Mongol way of life, including riding and hunting.

Planning for the Future

However, Genghis Khan did realize that he needed to make sure that someone would take over ruling his kingdom once he was gone. He could not choose his eldest son, Jochi, because he was not certain if he was Jochi's father, since the son was born soon after Borte had been kidnapped. Genghis Khan was a good judge of character, and he chose one of his other three sons, Ogedei, to inherit his kingdom after he was gone. He did specify that if Ogedei's children were not suitable to inherit the throne, then the role would be given to one of his other sons' children. He also divided his empire into several smaller territories, or khanates, with his other sons and grandsons ruling them under the authority of Ogedei.

The Death of the Great Khan

Genghis Khan now had an empire that, at that time, was the largest ever created. It stretched from the Caspian Sea to the Sea of Japan. He ruled over seven hundred cities and tribes. In 1226, Genghis Khan set out to fight the Tanguts in the Xi Xia kingdom again. An uprising there was threatening his control of the kingdom. That winter, he was crossing the Gobi Desert to attack the Tanguts when he stopped to hunt wild horses. His own horse panicked and threw Genghis Khan to the ground. He suffered internal injuries and developed a fever, but he refused to return home. The Mongol army captured the city of Tangut and reportedly killed its rulers and most of its citizens.

Six months later, Genghis Khan died, most likely from the injuries he had sustained during a hunt. No one is entirely sure what he died of. Some sources say he died of an illness, while others say it was the result of an arrow wound to the knee that became infected. He was about sixty-five years old. As he was dying, he told his son how to attack the Jin Empire in China, ordered the execution of the Tangut king, and told his advisers that his death must be kept secret if he died before the Tangut city surrendered.

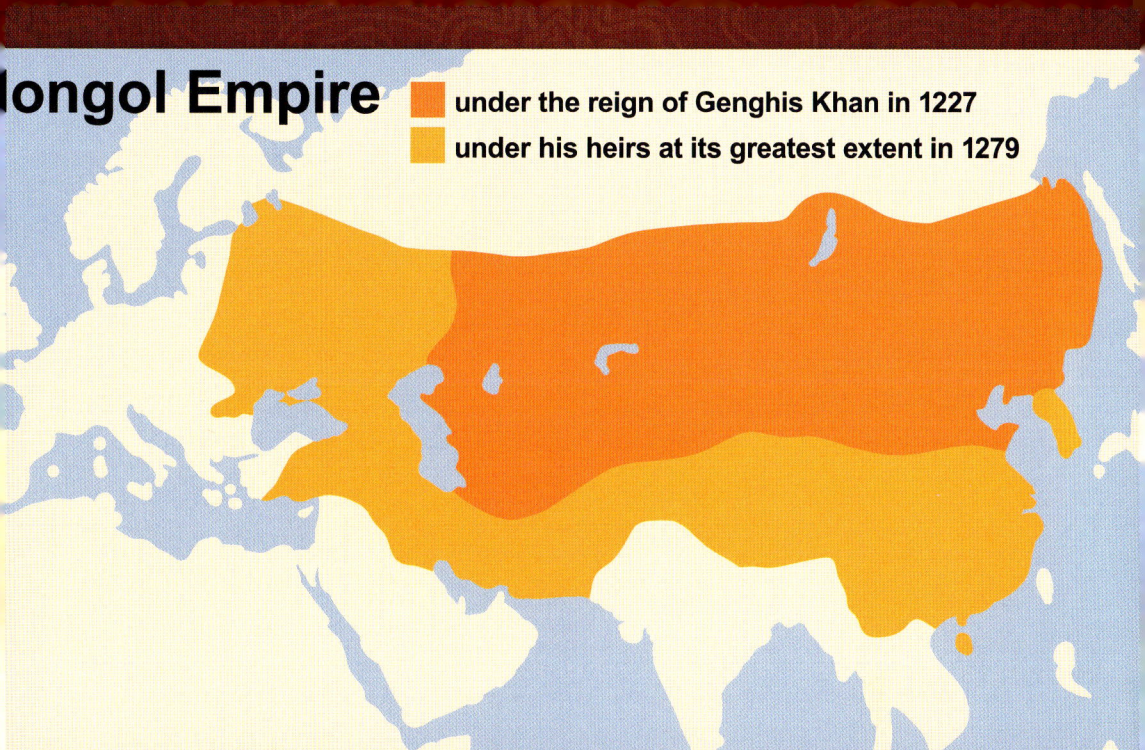

Mongol Empire   ◼ under the reign of Genghis Khan in 1227
◼ under his heirs at its greatest extent in 1279

This map shows Genghis Khan's Mongol Empire both in 1227 and later, at its largest size, in 1279.

A Secret Burial

Attendants cleaned the khan's body and dressed it in plain white robe, felt boots, and a hat. It was then wrapped in a white felt blanket perfumed with sandalwood and placed in a felt coffin with three golden straps. The body of Genghis Khan was returned to Mongolia, where it was buried on the sacred mountain of Burkhan Khaldun. The site was kept secret, and after the burial, herds of horses were driven over the grave to cover up any sign of it. Supposedly forty young girls and several horses were sacrificed there. Anyone involved in the

Finding Genghis Khan's Grave

People have been searching for Genghis Khan's grave almost since his death. He was rumored to have been buried with many priceless treasures. However, in 2015, the search for the grave went high tech. Searchers are now using satellite imaging. Because the area where Genghis Khan could be buried is so huge, researchers have used crowdsourcing to enlist ten thousand volunteers to help scan the eighty-four thousand images. They have identified fifty-five locations that have potential archaeological significance and might contain Genghis Khan's grave. However, many of the Mongolian people are angry about the quest to find their legendary leader's tomb. The site of the Great Khan's grave is considered to be a forbidden zone, and Mongolians do not want archaeologists disturbing their holy sites.

Genghis Khan's brutal invasions killed millions of people who farmed. Since large areas of Mongolia were no longer needed for farms, the land became forest.

burial was killed so as not to give away its location. After several years, no one even knew exactly where the grave was anymore.

Genghis Khan was dead. His son Ogedei was the new Great Khan. He reigned for twelve years, but when he died, there was another struggle for power. Eventually one of Genghis Khan's grandsons, Kublai, became the Great Khan. Kublai Khan carried on his grandfather's wishes and succeeded in uniting all of China under the Yuan dynasty. This was the first foreign dynasty ever to rule a united China. However, when Kublai Khan attempted to conquer Japan and southeast Asia, it eventually caused the collapse of the Mongol Empire into several different territories.

A Green Genghis

An unexpected legacy has made Genghis Khan one of the greenest invaders in history. Because he killed so many people (as many as forty million, according to some sources) during his brutal invasions, huge areas of land that had been farmed regrew as forests. Scientists in a Carnegie Institute study now believe that these regrown forests removed seven hundred million tons of carbon from the atmosphere. Many people think that humans only began impacting their environment when they started burning coal and oil. But any time when forests were cleared for farming, it made an impact on the earth because there were fewer trees to absorb carbon dioxide. So Genghis Khan's legacy also includes helping the earth, even though he never would have imagined it.

A Mixed Legacy

Genghis Khan is remembered as one of the most brutal military conquerors of all time. And yet he also introduced many enlightened methods of ruling, laws, and government systems that are used today. Like many legendary leaders, he was not all bad or all good, but a mixture of both.

In *The Secret History*, Genghis Khan's last words to his family were recorded as:

> *Acting to achieve some goal is the greatest of actions. A man who keeps his word will live with a mind that is strong. Keep your actions modest and supported by the people. Know the truth: your bodies too will someday pass on.*

Glossary

alliance A relationship formed for mutually beneficial reasons, especially between groups or countries.

aristocracy The highest social class in certain societies, sometimes based on family.

assassinate To kill an important person in a surprise attack, usually for political or religious reasons.

betrothed Engaged to be married.

clan A close-knit group of families who are usually related to each other.

crossbow A medieval bow that is attached to a wooden support and has a mechanism for pulling back and releasing the string.

decimal System of numbers based on the number ten, or on divisions into ten parts.

diplomat An official who represents his or her country, especially when traveling to another country for political reasons.

drought A period of time when not enough rain falls and water is in short supply.

dynasty A line of hereditary rulers of a country.

hereditary Based on family relationships or birth.

illiterate Unable to read or write.

khan A title given to rulers or officials, especially in central Asia.

kurultai A tribal council where clans and tribes make important decisions.

nomad A member of a group of people who constantly move from place to place instead of having a permanent home.

ordu A complex of yurts where a clan or tribal leader and his family live.

shaman A person, often a religious figure, who is said to have access to the spiritual world.

steppes A large area of flat grassland without trees, located in southeast Europe or Siberia.

Taoism A Chinese philosophy that values humility and religious piety.

trebuchet A catapult-like machine in which stones or other missiles are hurled by means of a weight attached to a short lever.

yurt A circular tent made of felt attached to a collapsible wooden framework.

For More Information

American Museum of Natural History
Central Park West at 79th Street
New York, NY 10024
(212) 769-5100
Website: http://www.amnh.org
The American Museum of Natural History's many exhibits include ones related to Genghis Khan and Mongolia.

The Franklin Institute
"Genghis Khan: Bring the Legend to Life"
222 N. 20th Street
Philadelphia, PA 19103
(215) 448-1200
Website: https://www.fi.edu/exhibit/genghis-khan
The Franklin Institute, a museum of science and science education, is the most recent host of this traveling exhibit on Genghis Khan and the Mongols.

International Museum of the Horse
"The Horse of the Steppes"
4089 Iron Works Parkway
Lexington, KY 40511
(800) 678-8813
Website: http://www.imh.org/exhibits/online/horse-steppes
This museum, dedicated to horses all over the world, features an exhibit on the horses specifically adapted to the environment of the steppes.

Royal Albert Museum
"Genghis Khan: Treasures of Inner Mongolia"
12845 102 Avenue NW
Edmonton, AB T5N 0M6
Canada
(780) 453-9100
Website: http://royalalbertmuseum.ca/exhibits/online/genghis/intro.htm
This museum's website features virtual exhibits and information from a past Genghis Khan exhibit.

Royal Ontario Museum
"A Warlord's Stronghold: Mystery on the Silk Road"
100 Queen's Park
Toronto, ON M5S 2C6
Canada
Website: https://rom.on.ca/en/exhibitions-galleries/exhibitions/a-warloard-stronghold-on-the-silk-road
This museum has a gallery of photographs and artifacts from the Silk Road and Genghis Khan's times.

Websites

Because of the changing nature of Internet links, Rosen Publishing has developed an online list of websites related to the subject of this book. This site is updated regularly. Please use this link to access the list:

http://www.rosenlinks.com/MON/genghis

For Further Reading

Adamson, Heather. *Mongolia* (Exploring Countries). Minneapolis, MN: Bellwether Media, 2016.

Aloian, Molly. *The Gobi Desert*. St. Catharine's, ON: Crabtree Publishing, 2012.

Bankston, John. *Genghis Khan* (Junior Biographies from Ancient Civilizations). Newark, DE: Mitchell Lane Publishers, 2013.

Bridges, Shirin Yim. *Sorghaghtani of Mongolia* (The Thinking Girl's Treasury of Real Princesses). Foster City, CA: Goosebottom Books, 2010.

Dittmar, Brian. *Mongol Warriors*. Minneapolis, MN: Bellwether Media, 2012.

Goldberg, Enid A. *Genghis Khan: 13th-Century Mongolian Tyrant*. New York, NY: Franklin Watts, 2009.

Helget, Nicole Lea. *Mongols* (Fearsome Fighters). Mankato, MN: Creative Education, 2012.

Krull, Kathleen. *Kubla Khan: The Emperor of Everything*. New York, NY: Viking Books for Young Readers, 2010.

Lewin, Ted, and Betsy Lewin. *Horse Song: The Naadam of Mongolia*. New York, NY: Lee & Low Books, 2014.

Medina, Nico. *Who Was Genghis Khan*? New York, NY: Grosset & Dunlap, 2014.

Nardo, Don. *Genghis Khan and the Mongol Empire*. Farmington Hills, MI: Lucent Books, 2010.

Pang, Guek-Cheng. *Mongolia* (Cultures of the World). New York, NY: Cavendish Square Publishing, 2010.

Bibliography

All Empires.com. "The Rise of Genghis Khan." January 2006. Retrieved April 4, 2016 (http://www.allempires.com/article/index.php?q=rise_of_genghis_khan).

Andrews, Evan. "10 Things You May Not Know About Genghis Khan." History.com. Retrieved April 29, 2014 (http://www.history.com/newshistory-lists/10-things-you-may-not-know-about-genghis-khan).

Biography.com. "Genghis Khan Biography." Retrieved November 15, 2015 (http://www.biography.com/people/genghis-khan-9308634).

Columbia University. "The Mongols in World History: Chinggis Khan." Asia for Educators. Retrieved November 15, 2015 (http://afe.easia.columbia.edu/mongols/figures/figures.htm).

Daily Mail. "Genghis Khan the GREEN: Invader Killed So Many People that Carbon Levels Plummeted." January 25, 2011. Retrieved April 4, 2016 (http://www.dailymail.co.uk/sciencetech/article-1350272/Genghis-Khan-killed-people-forests-grew-carbon-level-dropped.html).

De Hartog, Leo. *Genghis Khan: Conqueror of the World.* London, England: I.B. Tauris & Co. Ltd., 2004.

Duhaime Law Museum. "1206: The Yasak of Genghis Khan." January 3, 2009. Retrieved April 4, 2016 (http://www.duhaime.org/LawMuseum/LawArticle-519/1206-The-Yasak-of-Genghis-Khan.aspx).

The Field Museum. "Genghis Khan: Behind the Scenes." Retrieved November 15, 2015 (http://genghiskhan.fieldmuseum.org/behind-the-scenes).

Hays, Jeffrey. "Genghis Khan's First Conquest." Facts and Details, 2013. Retrieved November 15, 2015 (http://factsanddetails.com/asian/cat65/sub423/item2694.html).

Jarus, Owen. "Genghis Khan, Founder of Mongol Empire: Facts &

Biography." LiveScience.com, February 10, 2014. Retrieved April 4, 2016. (http://www.livescience.com/43260-genghis-khan.html).

Kahn, Paul, ed. *The Secret History of the Mongols: The Origin of Chingis Khan*. Boston, MA: Cheng & Tsui, 1998.

McCoy, Terrence. "The Frustrating Hunt for Genghis Khan's Long-Lost Tomb Just Got a Whole Lot Easier." *Washington Post*, January 8, 2015. Retrieved April 4, 2016. (https://www.washingtonpost.com/news/morning-mix/wp/2015/01/08/the-frustrating-hunt-for-genghis-kahns-long-lost-tomb-just-got-a-whole-lot-easier/).

Ratchnevsky, Paul. *Genghis Khan: His Life and Legacy*. Cambridge, MA: Blackwell, 1991.

Smith, Roff. "Genghis Khan's Secret Weapon Was Rain." National Geographic.com, March 12, 2014. Retrieved November 15, 2015 (http://news.nationalgeographic.com/news/2014/03/140310-genghis-khan-mongols-mongolia-climate-change).

Smitha, Frank E. "Genghis Khan and the Great Mongol Empire." Macrohistory.com. Retrieved November 15, 2015 (http://www.fsmitha.com/h3/h11mon.htm).

Weatherford, Jack. *Genghis Khan and the Making of the Modern World*. New York, NY: Crown Publishers, 2004.

INDEX

A
alliances, Mongol, 8, 13–14, 20, 22–23, 28, 29
andas (blood brothers), 12, 21, 23, 28, 30
aristocracy, 24
armies
    Chinese, 41, 43
    of Genghis Khan, 32, 38, 39–41, 44, 45, 46, 48, 50
    of Jamukha, 28
    of Temujin Khan, 21, 26, 28, 29

B
black bone lineage, 12
Bo'orchu, 20, 25
Borte, 14, 19, 20, 21, 23, 49

C
catapults, 41, 43, 44
clans, 10, 13–14, 15, 16, 17, 19, 27, 28, 32, 34
    alliances between, 20, 22, 30
    protection for, 23
crossbow, 44

D
Dei the Wise, 14

G
grave, of Genghis Khan, 51, 52, 53

H
Hoelun (mother), 10, 12, 15

horses, 6–7, 15, 19, 20, 22, 27, 38, 48, 49
    hunting of wild, 50
    importance to Mongol way of life, 12, 40
    sacrifices of, 51

J
Jamukha, 12–13, 21, 22–23, 27, 28, 29, 30
Jelme, 22
Jin Empire, 40, 41, 43, 46, 50
Jochi, 21, 49

K
Kara-Khitai, 46
Kasar, 15
Khwarizm dynasty, 43, 45, 46
kidnappings, 8, 10, 17, 23, 34, 49
Koyiten, battle at, 28
Kublai Khan, 53
kurultai, 16–17, 22, 30

M
Merkit tribe, 20, 21, 23

O
Ogedei, 49–50, 53
ordu, 24, 25, 26

S
shaman, 7–8, 37, 40
Silk Road, 41, 48
steppes, 6, 7, 8, 9, 16, 20, 23, 25, 28, 30
    tribes of the, 10, 14

T
Taichiud clain, 17, 19, 27, 28
Tangut kingdom, 40, 41, 50
Tatars, 8, 14, 27, 28
Tata-tonga, 34, 35
Teb Tengri, 7–8
Toghril, 21, 22, 23, 27, 28, 29–30
trebuchets, 43, 44

W
white bone lineage, 12

X
Xi Xia, 40–41, 46, 50

Y
Yassa, 34, 36
Yesugei (father), 10, 12, 14, 15, 23
yurts, 9, 24, 26

Z
Zhongdu, 41, 43

About the Author

Marcia Amidon Lusted has written 125 books and over 500 magazine articles for young readers. She is a former magazine editor and educator who lives in New Hampshire. She is fascinated by world history and loves writing nonfiction. Learn more about her books at http://www.adventuresinnonfiction.com.

Photo Credits

Cover, p. 3 (Genghis Khan) © iStockphoto.com/Josef Friedhuber; cover, p. 3 (map) © iStockphoto.com/Whiteway; interior pages background image (landscape) © iStockphoto.com/joyt; p. 7 © iStockphoto.com/Modilus; p. 11 National Palace Museum, Taipei, Taiwan/Bridgeman Images; p. 13 Wolfgang Kaehler/LightRocket/Getty Images; p. 16 AFP/Getty Images; p. 18 Print Collector/Hulton Archive/Getty Images; pp. 21, 26, 39 DEA/M. Seemuller/De Agostini/Getty Images; p. 24 Coprid/Shutterstock.com; pp. 29, 31 Bibliotheque Nationale, Paris, France/Bridgeman Images; p. 33 MPI/Hulton Fine Art Collection/Getty Images; p. 35 Pictures from History/Bridgeman Images; p. 38 Enrico Bortoluzzi/Shutterstock.com; p. 42 Science & Society Picture Library/Getty Images; p. 44 Fotosearch/Archive Photos/Getty Images p. 47 British Library, London, UK/Bridgeman Images; p. 51 Peter Hermes Furian/Shutterstock.com; p. 52 Dave Stamboulis/age fotostock/SuperStock

Designer: Matt Cauli; Editor: Meredith Day; Photo Researcher: Nicole DiMella